FINISHING LINE PRESS

www.finishinglinepress.com

Talmudic Verses

poems by

STEVEN SHANKMAN

Finishing Line Press
Georgetown, Kentucky

Talmudic Verses

ACKNOWLEDGMENTS

Publisher: Leah Huete de Maines
Editor: Christen Kincaid
Cover Art: a painting by Colette Brunschwig, from Arieh and Raphaël
Brunschwig, Les Amis de Colette Brunschwig (Friends of Colette
Brunschwig).
Author Photo: Jack Lui, Photographer
Cover Design: Elizabeth Maines McCleavy

Order online: www.finishinglinepress.com
also available on amazon.com

Author inquiries and mail orders:
Finishing Line Press
P. O. Box 1626
Georgetown, Kentucky 40324
U. S. A.

Table of Contents

For Colette Brunschwig

Children of Abraham: Shabbat 41a

"Didn't Rav Abba say that when anyone places his hands over his genitals it is as if he is denying the covenant of our father Abraham?"

Emerging from the river, Rabbi Zeira,
Naked, would stand up straight so all could see
That he was circumcised. Rav Ashi's school
Thought otherwise. When they went down to bathe
They stood up tall, but when they came back up
To face the others on the shore, they bent
Forward, with modesty. For them, to be
A child of Abraham was not to expose
Yourself, be seen. It was, instead, to be
Ashamed to fail to see the others' faces.

Master of Wings: Shabbat 49a

Why was Elisha called Master of Wings?
The Romans, when they ruled over the Jews,
Forbade *tefillin,* but Elisha, donning
His, in defiance, headed to the market.
Caesar's official saw him and, enraged,
Pursued him. Then Elisha, sensing danger,
Quickly removed his headgear. "What is that,"
The henchman shouted, "in your hand?" "A dove's
Wings," said Elisha. Skeptical, impatient,
The Roman waited, glaring at Elisha's
Closed fist. Elisha opened it. Behold,
A miracle! A dove's wings! Why a dove?
The house of Israel, the Rabbis say,
Is like a dove. As Scripture says, the children
Of Israel shall shine like a dove's wings
Covered in silver for, just as this dove
Is shielded only by its wings, so too
The Jewish people only find protection
By heeding the commandments. Miracle
Of miracles, that I shall love my neighbor
As if that loving were the very meaning
Of what it is to be myself, proclaiming
Peace to those far and near, always extending
The olive branch the dove brought to the ark,
To Noah's hand, after the flood subsided.

Miraculous Maternity: Shabbat 53b

A man's wife died. She just had given birth
To a son. The man was poor, could not afford
A wet nurse. Then, behold, a miracle!
The man grew breasts and nursed his son. "Come, see,"
Rav Yosef said, "the greatness of this man,
So great, he merited a miracle!"
Abaye, shocked, said, "How unnatural!"
Rav Nachman sided with the good Rav Yosef
As Shakespeare does when Lear dies of the mother,
His dear Cordelia in his arms, a man
At last, embodying maternity.

Pax Hebraica: Shabbat 63a

The Sages say a man may not go out
On Shabbos with a sword, nor with a bow,
Nor spear, nor club. But Rabbi Eliezer,
Considering these weapons decorations,
Says, since no Jew will ever use these arms
On Shabbos, or on any other day,
He may go out with them on Shabbos. "No!"
The Sages answer, shocked by the disgraceful
Image of Jews turning the Romans' arms
Into mere fashion. There is no true present
Not bending towards a messianic future,
A holy time of peace! The Sages cite
Isaiah: "They shall beat into plowshares
Their swords, to pruning hooks their spears. No nation
Will lift a sword against another nation.
They will no longer learn the ways of war."

Shoe Laces: Shabbat 66b

The synagogue faced our house, a constant presence,
and now my boyhood home is one.
I was close to my father, adored him, and he me.
He was warm, dignified, a healer with a bit
of a temper—familiar divine
attributes! He died
suddenly, too young, in his prime.
I was young—Joseph's age—seventeen,
and since then my life has been, it often seems,
a constant search for my father.
My father was secular, very,
but he was a bar-mitzvah and identified
as an M.O.T., as he put it,
a Member of the Tribe. I faithfully
honor the rituals, wrap myself
in *tefillin* most mornings, tightly
around my left arm and hand. Tightly.
It makes me feel close, feel at home,
think of home, my boyhood home,
across from the synagogue, a home
that is now an orthodox shul.

I went to services there on Shabbat
in my living room not long ago.
The rabbi gave me the honor
of leading the Torah service.
I opened the Ark—where my family's
mainly unused Bibles once lay on the bookshelf—
and removed the Torah, embraced it and carried it
around my living room. When I wrap
myself in *tefillin* I often
imagine my home, see the temple
from the large bay window of my living room,
a room that became a sanctuary,
and I feel serene and protected, close
to my father.

Today I read in the Talmud
about a young boy whose father—
to make his dear son's grief
at their inevitable
separation
more bearable—
would tie the string
from his right shoe to the son's left arm
so that the son, when he looked at the strings,
would feel close to his father
every time the son used his left arm,
and saw the familiar paternal
shoe laces, laces of the shoe
that did the father's walking, his
halachah,
and not on the right arm, the dominant arm,
for that would have reminded
the son too often
of his great grief,
of the vast
distance between
him
and his
father,
of the gravity of his
loss

Divine Spark: Shabbat 72b

What is idolatry? Am I permitted
To bow down to an idol if I bow
Out of respect for what my dear friend loves?
The Torah orders me to love my neighbor
As if that act of loving were itself
The very meaning of the self. So Rava
Asks, "Is it truly sinful to pay homage
To the other's ultimate concern?" A flicker
Of hope, a spark of the divine illumines
A dry stretch of these pages, threatens to
Set the surrounding text ablaze with love.

A Human Being: Shabbat 73a

Today is Thursday, time to write, to do,
And so I pen these novel lines to you.
On Shabbos I will rest and cease from newing,
A human being, not a human doing.

Creation Serves Me So That I May Serve: Shabbat 77b

Said Rav Yehuda, in the name of Rav,
"Of all the Holy One, Blessèd be He,
Created, not a single living thing
Is without purpose. Slug, fly, scorpion,
Mosquito, spider, snake have healing powers.
If a wasp stings you, crush a fly and spread
The fly paste on the sting. You will be cured."
All of creation made to serve my needs!
How flattering! And then we learn the fears
The weak provoke within the strong: the lion
Starts at the tiny polecat's piercing scream;
The mighty elephant is driven mad
By the mosquito deep inside its trunk.
Asked Rav Yehuda, in the name of Rav,
"What is the verse that clarifies these matters?"
Rav cites the prophet Amos: "the Almighty
Lifts the oppressed, the weak, over the strong."
Creation serves me so that I may serve
The weak, who trouble my complacency.

Holy Distance: Shabbat 87a

Sinai in smoky light
the ascent through a series
of near smoldering boundary stones
listen O Israel hear Me
O Moses
O Aaron
O *Kohanim*
O people
keep your holy distance
from the Holy Blessèd One *Ha Kadosh Baruch Hu*
so that you will be holy
and honor the holy distance
between you and the Other
and the Othermost Other
so that you and the Other and the Othermost Other
can approach each other through relation
and not assimilation
let your hand be open toward the Other
your brother
your sister
who are different like the digits
of the differing lengths
of the fingers of your open hand
not hidden in the sameness of a closed fist
as I am holy
so you be holy
holy you reaching out to Holy Me
hear O Israel
you did not hear
you cannot hear
the Other or the Othermost Other
when boundaries blur
Moses descends to
shouting mingling blind ecstasy the golden
calf

He smashed the Tablets, and the Holy One,

Blessèd be He, affirmed Moses' decision.
These Tablets "that you broke," *asher shibarta,*
As God told Moses, brings to mind the phrase
Yishar kochecha, "More power to you!"
So Reish Lakish says, hearing in *asher*
The word *iyshur,* or "affirmation." God
Affirmed his servant Moses' enterprise.
Only a separated self could rise
Out of this chaos to say "Here I am,
Ready to smash the Tablets You have carved
And then to carve a new set like the first ones."

We Will Do and We Will Hear: Shabbat 88a

When Israel accorded precedence
To "we will do" over "and we will hear,"
Consenting to receive the holy Torah,
The ministering angels came and tied
Two crowns to each and every Israelite.
So Rabbi Simai taught, and Rabbi Chana
Agreed, citing a verse from *Song of Songs:*
"Just like the apple tree among the trees
Of the forest" is God's love for Israel,
For as the fruit grows on an apple tree
Before its leaves appear, so did God's people
Say "we will do" before "and we will hear."
"You Jews are headstrong," said a naysayer,
"You leap before you listen, saying yes
To Torah, taking on the burden of
Responsibility before you weigh
The consequences of your hasty choice!"
Now in this time of plague, of distancing,
Of masks and calls for prudence, the brave young
And the incautious old, Israel's heirs,
Gather, a storm of holy protest, having
Seen the black face of innocence betrayed
While the brave young and the incautious old
Continue tending to the sick and dying.

Learning the Holy Alphabet: Shabbat 104a

The Rabbis told Yehoshua ben Levi:
First-graders came to study hall today
And said things unlike anything you have heard
Even from Joshua, the child of Nun,
Moses' disciple, who would never leave
His tent of study in the wilderness.
These children in the study hall explained
The sounds and the designs of Hebrew letters,
Taking them two by two and pondering
How each in every pair relates to the other,
Each child a Noah of the alphabet!
The first pair, *Aleph-Bet*, they said, means *Alaph
Bina*, "Learn wisdom," wisdom of the Torah.
The second pair is *Gimmel-Dalet,* meaning
Gemol Dalim, "you must give to the poor."
The *gimmel*'s leg, they said, is walking towards
The *dalet* as a kindly person seeks
The poor. So Abraham rushed from his tent
To welcome strangers in the heat of day,
Imploring them to stop and have a meal
Though Abraham, at ninety-nine, had just
Been circumcised, a child of Israel,
Feeling the pain of others as his own.

I Can't Breathe: Shabbat 105b

I am obliged to mourn, tradition states,
If the departed is a close relation:
Spouse, mother, father, daughter, sister, son.
Sensing that this is not quite right, the Rabbis
Ask whether I am not obliged to mourn
Not only relatives, but Torah scholars.
The Rabbis answer yes, though this might seem
A judgment tarnished by self-interest as
The Rabbis are all Torah scholars, so
They push ahead with yet another question.
If the deceased is not a Torah scholar
But is an upright person, must I mourn?
Yes, they decide. And what if I don't know
If he was righteous, but if I am standing
Over him as his soul departs, am I
Obliged to mourn for him? The Rabbis say
Yes, I must mourn for him as I must mourn
A Torah scroll that has been burned, for Torah
Teaches I must be loving towards my neighbor
As if that very loving were the meaning
Of "I," as in *Hineni*, "Here I am!"
If I am standing over him and hear
My neighbor utter "I can't breathe" and witness
His final breath, I am obliged to mourn
And even to protest, be it in a plague,
So the arc of history may bend toward justice.

Star Pupil: Shabbat 147b

Rabbi Elazar ben Arakh, the star
Pupil of Rabbi Yochanan ben Zakkai,
Moved to a town in Asia Minor famous
For soothing waters and the finest wine
But without Torah scholars. When their teacher
Passed on, Yochanan's other students moved
To Yavne. Elazar, no follower,
Awaited them in Asia Minor, but
They never came. He lived the good life there,
Went home, stood up, recited from the Torah
And misconstrued three letters in the verse
"This month shall be for you the first of months,"
A verse establishing the holiness
Of time that is inspired by the other.
He read, mistakenly, "Were their hearts mute?"
Did others truly exist for Elazar?
Elazar's colleagues, shocked by his misreading,
Prayed for God's mercy that his learning be
Restored. It was. What was the miracle
That freed his heart from error? Was it not
The back-and-forth of conversation with
His peers? I cannot study Torah on
My own. I need the other and the other
Others calling me into question, piercing
My self-sufficiency, my arrogance.

Abrahamic Faith: Shabbat 156b-157a

Rabbi Chanina says: "A constellation
Makes one wise, a constellation makes
One wealthy, and there is a constellation
For Israel." Yochanan disagreed,
Citing a verse from Jeremiah: "Thus
Says the Lord: 'Learn not the way of nations
And do not fear celestial signs.'" And Rav
Yehuda, citing Rav, famously stated,
"*Eyn mazel l'Yisrael*," there is no *mazel,*
No sign, no fate, no predetermined future
For Israel. Good deeds alone determine
The future. Abraham, an exile from
The East, his father an idolator,
Told God he was not fit to bear a son
According to the star charts he consulted.
"Exit astrology," the Lord commanded,
"*Eyn mazel l'Yisrael!*"; took him outside;
"Gaze heavenward and count the stars," He said.
"So shall your offspring be!" And Abraham
Trusted Him, and God reckoned this trust
Witnessed in Abraham as righteousness,
As the pursuit of justice, and more justice.

Teshuvah: Eiruvin 13b

i.
Why do the Sages rule for Beit Hillel
Over Beit Shammai? Beit Shammai are sharp,
Brilliant, their arguments airtight, exhaustive,
If stringent; Beit Hillel's more lenient, kind,
More generous. Both these and those, the Rabbis
Declare, bear witness to the living God,
To both rebuke and mercy, but Hillel
Always begins with deference to the views
Of Shammai. "Après vous, Monsieur!" they say
And so loving your neighbor won the day.

ii.
For two years and a half Beit Shammai and
Beit Hillel pondered if it would have been
Better had humans never been created.
Beit Shammai argued that it would have been
While Hillel said the world is better off
With human beings in it than with none.
They took a vote and finally concluded:

iii.
Never to have created Eve and Adam
Would have been best, the ancient Sages say.
Second best are repentant human creatures,
Each striving to be better every day.

Teaching: Eiruvin 54b

Rav Preida had a student who required
Four hundred repetitions of a teaching
Before he understood it. One day Rav
Was feeling called to take leave of his student
To attend to a matter that involved a *mitzvah*.
Rav taught his halting student the accustomed
Four hundred times, but still the student could not
Grasp the teaching. Rabbi Preida asked him,
"What's wrong today?" His student answered, "From
The very moment I became aware
That you were feeling obligated to
Perform a *mitzvah*, my attention slipped,
Worried that you would have to go too soon."
Then looking at the anxious face before him,
Rav Preida said, "Now listen to the teaching.
We will discuss it, then I will repeat it,
And will repeat it," which he did another
Four hundred times! And then a voice from heaven,
Astounded at Rav Preida's loving patience,
Offered the rabbi a reward. "Please choose,"
The voice said, "either to add four hundred years
To your life's span or for your generation
And you to merit places in the World
To Come." "I choose," Rav said, "that I and my
Generation merit places in
The World-to-Come." And then The Holy One,
Blessèd be He, replied to the angels: "Give him
Both this and this, both a long life - a life
Of loving service—and the calm assurance
He is a co-creator of a future
In which all learn to say 'thou' to another."

Only by Candlelight: Pesachim 7b-8a

The Sages taught: One does not search for leaven
By sunlight, moonlight, torchlight. Only by
Candlelight may one search the nooks and crannies
Of your own soul. The candle of Hashem
Searches through all the chambers of your insides,
Looking for puffiness, for the least trace
Of Pharaoh in your heart, for self-inflation.

Breakfast Times: Pesachim 12b

At what hour in the morning shall I eat?
It all depends on who you are. The first
Is for *Ludim,* gluttons who cannot wait.
Some say that these are hungry cannibals.
The second hour is the time for thieves
Who have been robbing others through the night
And take a nap before they seize their breakfast.
The third hour is for those with trust funds who
Can laze around and get up when they want to.
The fourth hour is for most of us. The fifth
Is for the working class who take their orders
From their employers and who therefore must
Delay their breakfast. In the sixth and final
Hour of the morning Torah scholars eat
Their first meal after having soaked themselves
In Torah. Torah teaches that we must
Welcome and feed the stranger and not eat him,
As the *Ludim* do and as does the Cyclops,
Flouting the rule of hospitality
Commanded by the Torah and by Homer.

Three Exceptions: Pesachim 25b

L'chayim, yes, but there are three exceptions.
Dying is better than engaging in
Adultery, murder, or idol worship.
If I commit adultery, I harm
The rightful partner of the adulteress.
If an official tells me, "Go and kill
That so-and-so, and if you don't, I will
Kill you!" you must resist, as Rava said:
"Let him kill you rather than you kill him."
Torah commands, "Thou shalt not kill." The other
Requires such deference. Idolatry,
Nearly convincing Abraham that he
Must murder Isaac, as if Moloch ruled,
Blurs the distinction between you and me.

Holy of Holies: Pesachim 26a

When it was necessary to repair
An item in the structure that contained
The Holy of Holies on the Temple Mount,
Hatches were opened in the upper story
And workers would be lowered in a crate
Closed on three sides so that their eyes could not
Feast on the beauties of the *cheruvim*
Facing each other, God's word in between.
Is it, perhaps, idolatrous to see
The holy separate from the face before me?

Clay Pots: Pesachim 30a

Rav said: "All clay pots used for cooking *chametz*
Before Pesach are now disqualified
Forever. You must shatter them!" Shmuel
Dissents from this strict ruling but he does so
Quietly, in deference to Rav,
The local rabbi. Suddenly the price
Of clay pots soared. Only the very rich
Could now afford them. Shmuel, incensed,
Told the pot merchants: "Stop your gouging now!
If you do not, I will be forced to announce
The lenient ruling of Rabbi Shimon
Who holds that you can keep these pots until
After *Pesach,* then use them as you wish."
Shmuel's deference to the other yields
To the demand of justice for the other
Others and for the other other others.

Dried Figs and Juicy Dates: Pesachim 31b-32a

If one unwittingly eats produce that
Is designated for a priest, one must
Repay the priest with the precise amount
The crop was worth when he mistakenly
Took it, and add a fifth to that amount.
Once, when I thoughtlessly consumed a priest's
Dried figs, then paid him back with juicy dates,
Which are worth more, the priest, to my surprise,
Rather than reprimand me for my sin,
Blessed me and said that God, blessèd be He,
Delights in acts of generosity.

Demons: Pesachim 111a

I thought that Judaism spelled the end
Of hocus-pocus, banishment of demons,
But now I read in *Pesachim* of demons
Everywhere! According to the Sages,
Three objects should not be allowed to pass
Between two people walking on a road:
A dog, a palm tree, and a woman, or
Some say a pig, some also say a snake.
And if these pass between me and my friend,
What is the remedy? Rav Pappa said:
"You should begin with *El* and then conclude
With *El*," that is, recite a pair of verses
That start with the word God and end with that
Same holy word, verses from *Bamidbar*,
The Book of Numbers, that insist that spells
Do not affect the Jewish people, that
The God who brought me out of Egypt made
Me free to make my own decisions, to
Create a holy future, not one given,
Decided in advance by demons who
Entice me back to slavery, to Egypt.

Rav Gidel's Teaching: Shekalim 7b

Rav Gidel said: the one who states a teaching,
Careful to cite the name of he who said it,
Should see the author of that teaching standing
Before him, face-to-face, in his mind's eye.
Language is not a system of abstract
Signs but words spoken to me by another.

Appeasing One Who Is Seen But Does Not See: Shekalim 15a

The great Rabbi Horshaya was the teacher
Of the son of a blind man. Every day
Rabbi Horshaya ate with the blind man.
One day Rabbi Horshaya had some guests
And did not dine with his blind friend or ask him
To join him and his guests to share a meal.
That evening Horshaya traveled up
To see the blind man and apologize.
"Please, master," said Hoshaya, "don't be angry
That I was absent earlier today
And missed our meal together. I had guests
And reasoned—please forgive me if I am wrong! –
That you, my master, might have felt embarrassed
To dine with strangers who are not accustomed
To dine with you." The blind man answered him:
"Since you have made this effort to appease
One who is seen but does not see, may you
Successfully appease," the blind man said,
"The Holy One who sees but is not seen."

Faith: Rosh Hashanah 4a

Does one who gives to charity so that
His child may live or so that he may merit
Life in the World-to-Come deserve the name
Of a full-fledged *tzaddik*, a righteous one?
Yes, the Gemara answers, if that person
Accepts, with equanimity, the outcome
With or without reward. Rashi agrees,
Adding that one who regularly gives
Without the expectation of reward
Is deemed a *tzaddik*. And a pious one?
Pirkei Avot states he who is expecting
To be rewarded for his charity
Stains the *mitzvah*. Faith is not a question
Of the existence or the non-existence
Of God. It is to adhere to the belief
That love without reward is valuable.

Difficult Freedom: Rosh Hashanah 9b

We are commanded in Leviticus:
"And you shall sanctify the fiftieth
Year and proclaim freedom throughout the land."
Rabbi Yehuda says if we don't sound
The *shofar*, it is still the Jubilee,
But "it shall be for you the Jubilee"
Means something is required to make it so,
According to Reb Yosei. He insists
We blow the *shofar* on the Jubilee,
That it will be the Jubilee if we
Fail to return the land to those who first
Owned it, and it will be the Jubilee
If we don't free our slaves, but the *shofar*'s
Necessary, piercing blasts declare
I am not free until we all are free.

Kimah Rising: Rosh Hashanah 11b-12a

The constellation *Kimah* which, some say,
Is a huge, curling dragon, when the flood
Began, instead of setting in the day,
Rose, as the Holy One, Blessèd Be He,
Removed two of its stars because the people
Sinned. Our father Abraham escaped
The shackles of astrology when he
Left Ur for an uncertain liberation
From a determined future. "Count the stars,"
God told him, if you can, for they are countless.
"So shall your offspring be," God said, the stars
Reflecting not determining a future
Influenced by the goodness of the people.

At What Point Were His Clothes Rendered Impure?: Yoma 67a

The person designated to dispatch
The goat for Azazel, that rocky, un-
Forgiving place, divided a red strip
Into two parts. He tied half to the rock
And tied the other half between the goat's
Two horns. Then making sure the goat could not
See where it was headed, turned the goat's
Body and face directly toward his own
And pushed it backwards. It went tumbling down,
Torn limb from limb before it reached the midpoint
Of its descent. Then the dispatcher walked
To the last booth of many that were placed
Along the route back to Jerusalem.
When it grew dark, he journeyed back to town
To purify himself. The Rabbis ask:
At what point were his clothes rendered impure?
Rabbi Shimon says: from the very moment
He faced the goat and shoved it off the cliff.

Blue Bloods: Yoma 71b

After the service in the Temple, those
Attending would escort the High Priest home.
Once, when the people saw Rabbis Shemaya
And Avtalyon, the heads of the Sanhedrin,
Walking along, in deference to their learning,
They left the High Priest and pursued the scholars,
Converts, it happened. High Priests, unlike Rabbis,
Ascend through lineage to their positions,
Blue bloods whose learning often was not deep.
Shemaya and Avtalyon approached
The High Priest wishing to bid him farewell.
Jealous of the attention that the people
Paid to Avtalyon and to Shemaya,
The High Priest told the Rabbis: "May you scions
Of the *goyim* come and go in peace!"
The Rabbis answered the High Priest in turn:
"Better that the descendants of the nations
Should come, like Aaron, in a spirit of peace
Than that descendants of the peaceful Aaron
Not practice Aaron's peaceful practices."

Holy Interruption: Yoma 85a-85b

If a man comes intently toward his neighbor
And slays him, be that man a priest, and later
Performs his priestly duties in the Temple,
High on God's altar, you should not remove him
To execute him for his mortal crime
Until he finishes the Temple service.
But if a priest can offer testimony
Confirming the innocence of someone who,
Just at that moment, stands before a court
Weighing the penalty of death, you must
Interrupt, without delay, the Temple
Service since doing so can save a life.

Toward the Other: Yoma 87a

The Mishnah states: the sins of man toward God
Will be atoned for on the holy day
Of Yom Kippur, but for my sins against
Others, I must approach the one I hurt
And speak with them and ask for their forgiveness.
But Rav Yosef bar Chavu disagrees.
If a man sins, he says, then Elohim
Will reconcile. Why Elohim and not
The Tetragrammaton, *Yod-He-Vav-He*?
Elohim means the judge. Justice appeases
The offended party. No need for the sinner
To approach the victim and apologize!
For Levinas, the text of the Gemara
Rises up against Rav Yosef's way
Of ranking the universal order over
The interpersonal. No, the offended
Person must always be appeased, approached,
Consoled. For what is God, asks Levinas,
If not the permanent refusal of
A history indifferent to our tears?
A world without such acts of consolation
Will never be at peace. The harmony
With God can only be achieved by me
When I approach the Other, say I'm sorry.

Who is Here?: Sukkah 53a

Hillel the Elder was rejoicing at
The place of the Rejoicing of the Drawing
Of Water. He said this: "If I am here,
Then everyone is here. And if I am
Not here, then who is here?" Some say that God
Utters these words, but I say God is born
Witness to by these holy words, for who
Am I, I truly, if not he who says
Hineni, "Here I am! I am the one
Who is responsible. I cannot wait
For no one to step forward. Here I am!"

Yin and Yang: Beitzah 20a

Beit Shammai say you need not place your hands
On the head of the animal that stands
Before you just before its sacrifice.
Beit Hillel say you must. Which will suffice?
The Sages taught: there was an incident
Involving Hillel, who had brought his burnt
Offering to the Temple. Hillel placed
Both his hands firmly, bending at the waist,
On the head of the animal he brought.
Beit Shammai rushed to encircle him. They sought
A confrontation, certain that Hillel
Had brought a male. Hillel, knowing full well
Burnt offerings are always male, then swung
The creature's tail in front of them, who had clung
To their conviction that this was a male
And that their point of view had to prevail.
Real men must always win! They cannot fail!
The wildly swinging tail obscured their vision,
Allowing Hillel to offer a revision
Of naked truth. "A female, and a peace
Offering," he said, "I've brought." Male energies,
Less threatened, calmed. Beit Shammai left. Hillel,
Gentle and loving, bid them each farewell.

To What Strangers, What Welcome?: Beitzah 32a

Rav Natan bar Abba said that Rav said:
The wealthy Jews of Babylonia
Are bound to go hell if they are not
Compassionate. Shabbetai bar Marinus
Happened to come to Babylonia.
The name Marinus, with its Latin ring,
Struck the Jews strangely, and in fact repelled them.
He asked for work but they refused to hire him.
He begged for food. They did not give him any.
Shabbetai bar Marinus, he of mixed
Ancestry, said these wealthy Jews must be
Descendants of the *erev rav*, the mixed
Multitude, not of the very few
Chosen to take responsibility
For others, open-hearted and beloved
Of God. Those who are merciful are truly
Descendants of our father Abraham.
Even our father was not Abraham
When he expelled Hagar *ha ger*, the stranger,
And Ishmael to what strangers, to what welcome?

Thou Shalt be Gentle: Ta'anit 20a-20b

The Sages taught: you must be pliable,
Soft like a reed, not stiff like a tall cedar.
Rav Elazar, son of Rabbi Shimon,
Strolling along a river bank, was glowing,
Full of himself for knowing so much Torah.
His self-regard was interrupted by
A man Rav Elazar deemed unattractive,
And had the nerve to tell him so. The man
Rebuked him. Recognizing he had sinned,
Rav Elazar begged for the man's forgiveness
And finally the offended man relented,
Accepting Elazar's apology.
Rav Elazar then rushed to the yeshiva
To teach the precious Torah he had learned:
"A person should be always like a reed,
Soft and not stiff like cedars, which is why
The quills of Torah scribes are drawn from reeds,
For Torah teaches gentleness, not pride."

Worthies of the World-to-Come: Ta'anit 22a

Four souls are worthy of the World-to-Come:
The prison guard who puts his life at risk
To save a Jewish maiden from a rapist;
The one who, when he hears of a decree
Against the Jewish people, tells the Rabbis
So they can pray for mercy and annul it;
And two Jewish comics who cheer up
The sorrowful among us in this too
Sad and contentious world longing for peace.

The Spirit of Holiness: Megillah 7a

"Establish me for future generations!"
So said Queen Esther of Megillah fame
Before the Book of Esther was included
In Holy Scripture. Shmuel contended
It lacked the sanctity of other scrolls.
Was this because the Holy One is never
Mentioned by name in all of the Megillah?
But what is holiness if not to place
My life at risk to stand against injustice?
The Holy One's transcendence to the point
Of absence means I am responsible.

Reading Torah in Greek: Megillah 8b

Parchments in ritual objects like *tefillin*
And *mezuzot* are written in the sacred
Language, in Hebrew and in Hebrew script,
While Torah scrolls are written in all tongues.
Rabban Shimon ben Gamliel insists
That Torah scrolls be written only in Greek,
Language of universals, for the Torah
Is true because it speaks to everyone.

The Ethics of Attribution: Megillah 15a

And Rabbi Elazar said that Chanina
Had said whoever says a saying in
The name of he who said it brings redemption
To the whole world, for deference to the other
Redeems the world. Seizing false credit dooms it.

Light is Sown for the Righteous: Megillah 24a-24b

One who is blind may say the prayers and blessings
Preceding the *Shema*. Rabbi Yehuda
Objects, insisting one who has not seen
The heavenly light of sun and moon and stars
And benefited from them cannot praise them.
The Rabbis disagree. They follow Rabbi
Yosei, who all his life was puzzled by
The verse from Deuteronomy that reads,
"And you shall grope at noon just as the blind man
Gropes in the darkness," understanding this
To mean the blind man struggles in the night
More than he does in daylight. Then one night
Rabbi Yosei came upon a blind man
Holding a torchlight and he asked: "My son,
Why do you need this torch, since you are blind?"
"So others can see me," he said. "They save me
From stumbling into pits and thorns. For this
Light sown for the righteous I am grateful!"

The Way Up and the Way Down is the Same: Megillah 31a

Said Rabbi Yochanan: "Whenever Scripture
Extols God's might, you will then find a mention
Of His humility. The Torah states:
'God is the God of gods, seeking out justice
For the orphan and the widow.' In the Prophets
We read: 'Thus says the High and Lofty One
Whose name is holy and who dwells on high
And with the humble and contrite.' And in
The Writings it is written: 'He who rides
Upon the clouds exalt, Whose name is Ya,
Father of orphans, widows' staunch defender.'"

To Excommunicate or Not to Excommunicate: Moed Katan 17a

There was a learned Torah scholar who
Was held in ill repute. "What should we do?"
The Rabbis asked. "To excommunicate him
Is not an option, for if we berate him,
The name of Heaven is besmirched. Besides,
We need his learning!" *Malachi* provides
A verse that teaches that a teacher is
A holy messenger, that we must busy
Ourselves with Torah from the mouths of angels,
For I am present in the words I speak,
So Rav Yehuda ostracized that scholar.
Before he left this world, Yehuda laughed,
Giddy he had resisted flattering
Learning that was not moral at its core.

Responsibility for the Other: Chagigah 15

Acher, the Other, having gone astray,
Asked Rabbi Meir, "What's the meaning of
The verse: 'God has created even this
And this?'" Meir responded, "Even those
Who deem themselves unrighteous can become
Righteous, if they repent." Then Acher said,
"But have I not already told you that
I heard, behind the curtain of the world,
A voice that said 'Return, rebellious children,
Except for Acher'"? But Rabbi Meir
Would not give up on Acher, for I am
Responsible for Acher, for the Other,
Even for his responsibility.

My Table Atones for Me: Chagigah 27a

The sacrifices are idolatry.
From a verse in Ezekiel we see
The truth of this. The verse begins with "altar"
And ends with "table," meaning, when I falter,
My table atones for me as I receive
My needy guests, granting me a reprieve.

A Certain Roman Matron: Rosh Hashanah 19a

At four times of the year the world is judged.
On Passover, judgment is passed concerning
Grain; on Shavuot judgment is passed
Concerning fruits; on Rosh Hashanah all
God's creatures pass before Him just like sheep
And on Sukkot we are judged concerning water,
If we shall live in drought or blessed by rain.
Four days of judgment and four Rosh Hashanahs,
Two Talmuds, each with Mishnahs and Gemaras.
Gemaras and Gemaras and Gemaras
And Rabbis who agree and disagree,
A plethora of voices and opinions
Always ascribed to someone, to Rav Yosef
Or Rav Kahana or Rabbi Yitzhakh.
Why did the Talmud not identify
The Roman matron who advised the Jews
When Rome forbade studying Torah and
Circumcision and Shabbat observance?
"Come and cry out at night," she urged them, "startle
Those in the streets and shops, imploring them,
'Are you and we not children of the same
Father and mother? Hath not a Jew eyes?'"
Recalled to *chesed*, to *humanitas*
By one left nameless by the Rabbis, Rome
Revoked its harsh decrees. Does the absence of
Her proper name suggest rabbinic slight
Or that true virtue is its own reward
Or loving caution for the sake of those
Who, once identified as benefactors,
May find themselves at future deadly risk?

NOTES

These poems reflect on passages from several tractates of the massive, truly oceanic Babylonian Talmud. There are two Talmuds: the Jerusalem Talmud and the Babylonian Talmud, which is the more voluminous and is considered the more authoritative of the two. The Babylonian Talmud consists of the Mishnah, compiled by Rabbi Judah Ha-Nasi around 220 CE; and the Gemara, dated roughly three hundred years later than the Mishnah, which comments on the Mishnah.

Master of Wings: Shabbat 49a

Tefillin consist of two small black boxes with leather straps, one wrapped around the arm and the other around the head, that are worn during prayer.

Shoe Laces: Shabbat 66b

A *halachah* means a legal ruling. It is derived from the verb *halak,* meaning "to walk."

We Will Do and We Will Hear: Shabbat 88a and I Can't Breathe: Shabbat 105b

Both poems refer to the murder of George Floyd, a 46-year-old African-American man, at the hands of Derek Chauvin, a 44-year-old white police officer, in Minneapolis on May 25, 2020, in the midst of the COVID-19 pandemic and the nation-wide protests that followed in the wake of Floyd's murder.

Holy Distance: Shabbat 87a

Kohanim are priests.

Teshuvah: Eiruvin 13b

Teshuvah, or "repentance," literally means a "return" (to God).

"Beit Hillel" is the school (literally, the "house") of Rabbi Hillel.

"Après vous, Monsieur!" means "After you, Sir!" Emmanuel Levinas was fond of saying that this phrase sums up his thought.

Teaching: Eiruvin 54b

A *mitzvah* is a divine command.

Three Exceptions: Pesachim 25b

L'chayim means "to life."

Holy of Holies: Pesachim 26a

Cheruvim (plural of *cheruv*, or *cherub*) are the two celestial, winged beings (Exodus 25:20) that face each other on the holy Ark.

Clay Pots: Pesachim 30a

Pesach is Passover.

Faith: Rosh Hashanah 4a

Pirkei Avot ("Chapters of the Fathers") is a famous compilation of rabbinic ethical teachings.

Lines 15-16: "the belief/That love without reward is valuable." In "The Paradox of Reality," Emmanuel Levinas writes: "Faith is not a question of the existence or non-existence of God. It is believing that love without reward is valuable."

Difficult Freedom: Rosh Hashanah 9b

Difficult Freedom [Difficile liberté]: Essays on Judaism is the title of a book by Levinas that is comprised exclusively of many of his writings about Judaism.

Toward the Other: Yoma 87a

"Toward the Other" (*Envers autrui*) is the title of Emmanuel Levinas's essay on a passage from the tractate *Yoma* (47a-88a).

To What Strangers, What Welcome?: Beitzah 32a

To What Strangers? What Welcome? is the title of a series of poems by J. V. Cunningham.

The Spirit of Holiness: Megillah 7a

In his essay "God and Philosophy," Levinas says that the God of the Hebrew Bible is "transcendent to the point of absence" (*transcendant jusqu'à l'absence*).

Reading Torah in Greek: Megillah 8b

Mezuzot is the plural of *mezuzah*, a piece of parchment contained in a decorative case that is hung on the doorpost of Jewish homes.

The Ethics of Attribution: Megillah 15a

In Mark Kramer's *Telling True Stories: A Nonfiction Writer's Guide from the Nieman Foundation at Harvard University* (Penguin Publishing Group, 2007), the section on ethics, written by Roy Peter Clark, is entitled "the ethics of attribution." Hence the title of this poem. My thanks to Peter Laufer for this reference.

Light is Sown for the Righteous: Megillah 24a-24b

Shema (meaning "Listen!") is the first word of Judaism's central prayer ("Listen, Israel! *Adonai* is our God, *Adonai* alone!").

Responsibility for the Other: Chagigah 15

In Chapter 8 of *Ethics and Infinity*, Levinas says, of the Other, that "I am responsible for his very responsibility."

A Certain Roman Matron: Rosh Hashanah 19a

Chesed is loving-kindness.

Acknowledgements

Tikkun Magazine: "A Human Being: Shabbat 73a," "We Will Do and We Will Hear: Shabbat 88a," "Learning the Holy Alphabet: Shabbat 104a," "I Can't Breathe: Shabbat 105b"

Many of these poems were inspired by the writings of Emmanuel Levinas, who is justly famous for the originality and daring of his Talmudic readings.

I wish to express my enduring gratitude to Colette Brunschwig, to whom this book is dedicated, for her friendship and for so generously hosting - in her charming apartment on rue Poussin in Paris not far from the École normale Israélite orientale where Emmanuel Levinas taught and served as principal for many years - our lively sessions of Talmud study on Shabbat afternoons.

Thanks to Arieh and Raphaël Brunschwig of "Les Amis de Colette Brunschwig" for their generous permission to reproduce the work of art (India ink on paper, untitled and undated) by Colette Brunschwig that graces the cover of this book. That work is a gift from the artist to me and my wife, Marsha Maverick Wells, who curated the exhibition "Brush in Hand: Ink Wash Paintings by Colette Brunschwig" at the White Lotus Gallery in Eugene, Oregon in spring of 2007. I am grateful to Hue-Ping Lin, the gallery's owner, for presenting that remarkable show. My enduring thanks to Jeffrey Librett and Dawn Marlin for introducing me to Colette and her paintings.

Thanks to Jack Liu for his photograph of Colette Brunschwig's painting, as well as for his photograph of this book's author.

I am especially grateful to Leah Huete de Maines of Finishing Line Press for her welcoming of this book. For their receptiveness to these poems, and for their gracious feedback, my sincere thanks, as well, to Richard Argosh, Judith Baskin, Barbara Bundy, Marjorie Feldman, Ken Fields, Karen Ford, Sandy Goodhart, Evlyn Gould, Rabbi Yitzhak Husbands-Hankin, David Hansel, Joëlle Hansel, Esther Jacobson-Tepfer, Gareth Reeves, David Richman, Rabbi Ruhi Sophia Motzkin Rubenstein, Lynn Schwartz, Rabbi Alyson Solomon, Tim Steele, Dick Stein, Gary Tepfer, Rosanna Warren, Marsha Maverick Wells, Ingrid Wendt, Mark Whalen, and Lucy Zammarelli.

I am grateful to my Talmud teachers in Paris, Georges Hansel and Yves Sobel, as well as to Rabbi Jacob Siegel in Eugene; and to my Talmud study partners Oriana Kahn Hurwit, Luba Jillings, Gordon Lafer, and Debbie and Shlomo Libeskind.

STEVEN SHANKMAN holds the UNESCO Chair in Transcultural Studies, Interreligious Dialogue, and Peace and is co-director of the UNESCO Crossings Institute at the University of Oregon, where he is Distinguished Professor Emeritus of English and Classics. Before coming to Oregon, he taught at Princeton, Columbia, and Harvard.

His work in the Western classical tradition includes *Pope's Iliad: Homer in the Age of Passion* (1983) and *In Search of the Classic: Reconsidering the Classical Tradition, Homer to Valéry and Beyond* (1994). His Penguin edition of Pope's *Iliad* appeared in 1996. Some of his later work, including *The Siren and the Sage: Knowledge and Wisdom in Ancient Greece and China* (co-authored with Stephen Durrant, 2000) and *Early China/Ancient Greece: Thinking through Comparisons* (co-edited by Stephen Durrant, 2002), compares classical traditions. With Stephen Durrant and four others, he is an editor of *The World of Literature* (1999), an anthology of world literature from a global perspective, which contains some of his own poetic translations from Chinese, Greek, and Latin. He is the author of two books of poems: his chapbook *Kindred Verses* (2000) and *Talmudic Verses* (2023). His poetry has appeared in a number of journals including *Tikkun, Sewanee Review, Literary Imagination, Literary Matters,* and *Poetica Magazine. Epics and Other Higher Narratives: An Intercultural Approach,* co-edited by Amiya Dev, appeared in 2010, as did his book *Other Others: Levinas, Literature, Transcultural Studies.* He has been a Guggenheim and an NEH Fellow.

His most recent scholarly book is *Turned Inside-Out: Reading the Russian Novel in Prison* (Northwestern University Press, 2017). He is currently at work on a translation from the French of *Suerte: L'exclusion volontaire,* a semi-autobiographical novel (1995) by Claude Lucas, the so-called "gangster philosopher" who, before writing *Suerte,* became a devotee of Emmanuel Levinas's first magnum opus, *Totality and Infinity;* and a study of Levinas and Tolstoy.

www.ingramcontent.com/pod-product-compliance
Lightning Source LLC
Chambersburg PA
CBHW030309100426
42812CB00002B/638